A LITTLE SOMETHING

SELECTED POEMS AND PROSE
BY

RICHARD EDWARD NOBLE

A Little Something

Poetry and Prose

RICHARD EDWARD NOBLE

First Edition

ISBN 978-0-9798085-3-1

Published in the United States of America
by
Noble Publishing, 889 C. C. Land Rd., Eastpoint, Fl. 32328.

Cover, layout and design by
Graphic Designer, Diane Beauvais Dyal

Interior, layout and design by
Carol Noble

CONTENTS

LOVE AND OTHER NICE THINGS

TENDERNESS AND TEARS

ON THE SERIOUS SIDE

INTRODUCTION

About the Author

Richard Edward Noble was born in Baltimore, Md. at St. Agnes Hospital in the year 1943. As a baby he was relocated to Lawrence, Massachusetts, the home of his parents and their relatives.

He attended St. Rita's Grammar School, Central Catholic High School, Northern Essex Community College in Haverhill, and Merrimack College in North Andover.

His mother, father, and grandparents - on both sides of the family - were textile workers.

Richard lived in Lawrence until the age of twenty-seven. He then migrated to Fort Lauderdale, Florida. He started his career in the food service industry at the New England Oyster House restaurant chain working as a dishwasher/porter. In less than a year he was managing the restaurant.

Richard met his wife Carol at that same restaurant on Sunrise Blvd. She was a waitress/barmaid.

After a number of frustrating years in the restaurant business, Carol and Richard decided that they needed more adventure in their lives. They purchased a van and remodeled it themselves. They then resigned their positions and went off on an adventure to see America. Their travels resulted in Richard's first book Hobo-ing America - a book filled with humor and the pathos and frustration of the poor itinerant worker.

As a result of this adventure they ended up in the Florida Panhandle in the small town of Eastpoint harvesting oysters in

Apalachicola Bay. After more than a decade of oyster harvesting, Richard and Carol opened a small business on the outskirts of the neighboring community of Carrabelle. They spent another decade selling ice cream cones and sandwiches in Carrabelle and then sold their business and retired.

Richard now works as a freelance writer. He has a column in one of the local newspapers called the Eastpointer. It is focused on local issues relating to his experiences in the Eastpoint oystering community and life in the small town of Eastpoint. He won a first place award for humor from the Florida Press Association.

Richard writes every day. He has started his own publishing company and publishes his own creations. This book of poems will be his fourth creation. His other books are listed elsewhere. He also writes a popular blog called the Hobo Philosopher. His blog contains his Eastpointer columns and is primarily educational. He publishes book reviews and his research on a variety of subjects which include: philosophy, history, economics, political science, the history of unionism in America, biographies of famous people and historical essays.

ALSO BY
RICHARD EDWARD NOBLE

HOBO-ING AMERICA
A workingman's tour of the U.S.A.

A SUMMER WITH CHARLIE
A story about the last days of a young sailor.

HONOR THY FATHER AND THY MOTHER
A tragic novel.

MY

HOMETOWN

MY HOMETOWN

My hometown, like every hometown has a history. The history of Lawrence, Massachusetts involves the industrial revolution. Lawrence was a mill town and, in part, still is today. For my early life and long before I was born, they manufactured textiles there. Lawrence is the story of women working, and their battle for rights. Lawrence is the story of unions and labor riots. Lawrence is the story of boom and bust. Lawrence is not an example of America. Lawrence is America.

Lawrence is Emma Lazarus's words inscribed on the base of the Statue of Liberty, in their raw, plain reality. In Lawrence, growing up, I met the whole north, south, east, and west of Europe. In Lawrence, I met every language and every ethnic, but only one ethic - hard work.

I am glad that I had the opportunity to grow up in Lawrence. Lawrence is unlike any other place in America that I have ever been, and I've been almost everywhere in this United States. In Lawrence, without even realizing it, I learned to take pride in work and not look at it as a curse of a lower class. In Lawrence I absorbed, color, race, nationality, ethnic background, and difference, as the skin absorbs vitamin D from sunshine. I have friends whose names end in vowels and consonants.

I must be honest, I really didn't think much of good, old Lawrence while I was there, but now that I have seen a bunch of elsewhere, I realize what a place it was. It is like none other, and a very large part of what I am, I inherited from Lawrence - My Home Town!

MY HOMETOWN

My hometown, as I remember, was poor and broke.

The streets were a patchwork of potholes and tar,

Three tenement houses, and out front ... an old car.

My hometown, as I remember, and it fills me with pride,

Was filled with calloused hands and blue collared shirts,

Not soft palms waiting to be greased

And phony smiles wearing suits and ties.

My hometown was telephone poles, see-saws and swings.

My hometown was streets full of kids and be home before dark.

My hometown, as I remember, was bowling alleys and draft
      beer.

My hometown, it was cheep and it was poor.

My hometown, it was old ... it was weary ... it was sore.

My hometown, it was crusty rye bread and oleo.

My hometown was salt pork, potatoes, and stew.

My hometown, as I remember, wasn't very sweet.

It wasn't indoor cats and walks for dogs.

It wasn't a piece of cake.

My hometown though, as I remember, wasn't all that bad.

My hometown though, as I remember, wasn't all that sad.

My hometown was a bit of a joke, and a good deal of smoke,

But never a pig in a poke.

It was true workingman blue,

And they'll spit in your eye if you say that's a lie.

My hometown, as I remember, wasn't shiny fenders on antique
cars.

It was more brass rails and poorly lit bars.

Actually, my hometown, as I remember, it was kind of nice.

It was somewhat friendly and sort of warm,

But, I think it's gone;

That is, my hometown ... as I remember.

HANGIN' OUT

It was a long, long time ... a long, long time,
That we were all just one of the guys
Just hangin' out, sittin' up on the wall.

Just hangin' out ma, just hangin' out!

Sometimes we were just there.
Sometimes it was a ball.
Now I'm older and that's all the past.
Often I wonder if it's my memory's lapse,
Or did I really know any of those guys.
We're they really pals, buddies, friends?
Their memory gets fuzzy.
I tell myself that there's only today.
They never knew me, and I never knew them.
They're just a bunch of ghosts in my memory's way.
But then when I'm huddled in one of those lonely corners
With all the dark shadows, hard knuckles and calloused hearts,
I hear a sigh, a creek, a crack, a cry,
And then there's a tear in my eye.
I see a laughing face, then feel a slap on my back.
It could be Tom, or Dutch, Chucky or Jack.
And all of a sudden,
I'm up on the Corner. I'm on the wall.

I'm hangin' out ma, just hangin' out.

I'm on the corner;

I'm in Costy's yard.
I'm down at Nel's;
Or in Michaud's back seat.
I'm up Joe's cellar;
Or behind the Social - a little stick ball,
Or down the beach.
I'm just standin' on the Corner
Or in the middle of Lawrence Street.

I'm hangin' out ma.

I'm just hangin' out with my friends, my buddies.
Up on the corner.

Hangin' out ma, just hangin' out.

I'm up the Corner.
I'm on that old bench.
Hangin' out.
I'm with my old buddies.

I'm hangin' out ma, just hangin' out...
I'm just hangin' out.

SIDE OF THE ROAD

When you live your life by the side of the road,
You always know which way the traffic flows.

When you live your life by the side of the road,
You see their faces but not their toes.

You might catch a glint, a gleam, or a sparkle,
You might even think that you know who they are.

But when you live your life by the side of the road,
What you really know, is which way the traffic goes.

You will see them talking and laughing inside,
And maybe children bouncing about on a back seat.

You see the mustaches, the braids, the balding heads.
You see them staring, lost in thought.

But from the side of the road, you can't see their toes,
And all you know, really, is which way the traffic flows.

From the side of the road you can watch the race,
You can dodge the traffic when you know it's safe.

From the side of the road you don't need a car,
You can walk on the shoulder or follow a star.

You can watch the lights and read the signs.
You can walk or don't walk.

You can sleep under a bridge;
You can make your own mind.

But from the side of the road you can't see their toes,
And all you know, really, is which way the traffic flows.

From the side of the road the lights at night can get bright
And speeding traffic can buzz in your ears.

From the side of the road things can often get hazy,
A blur, a maze; one can get lost, and even go crazy.

From the side of the road, there is no place to go.
You never know the things that 'they' know,

Or where they come from, or where they go,
And you never see the tips of their toes.

And all you know, really, is the way the traffic flows.

SUNDAY ON THE CORNER

The sun shines warmly, as the wind cools,
Making the morning shine briskly.
The streets are still wet.
The sun sparkles in the tiny holes of the black tar.
Not like the stars in the dark and distant night shining,
Instead it glistens with a sparkle that's simple.
A sparkle of warmth and happiness.
The sparkle in a friend's eyes, as tears from laughter moisten,
And blur all the smiling faces standing by,
And every color appears as if for the first time.
Yellows bright, and blacks from Cadillacs
With the reflection of the world seen in every fender.
The tops of buildings,
And the refracted poles and streetlights,
And smiling faces laughing by the mailbox,
As friends meet and greet
And pass the morning in pleasant conversation.

First the family.
The face of a woman, galled and set,
With a wetness that only tears beget.
She sits up straight and stares ahead.
"Why? ... Why is he dead?"
Her face folds up into her hands.
Her elbows rest on her knees.
But before her eyes she sees...
She sees his smile ... and hears his voice.
But all that can really be heard are the bursts of her sobs

As they fill the solemn freshness,
Of the grey upholstered limousine.

The driver sits in his stripped tuxedo.
His smooth grey gloves clench the wheel.
"Die, die ... why must he die? Why can't it be me?"
She says to herself as she raises her head.
Her handkerchief held delicately to her raw, irritated nose.
And down the street the black limousine goes...
And another ... and another ... and another.
And then a line of blues and grays and greens...
Bright and clean ... every headlight bearing a faint yellow
        gleam.
All is as it seems.
The sun still sends its beams,
And children still have their dreams.
The mailbox is red and blue,
And the sky is too.
And beauty, with a sigh, needs no reason why...

No reason why.

THERE'S A MAN IN MY LIFE

There's a man in the doorway with a brown paper sack.

There's a man at the window.

I can just see his back.

There's a man in the kitchen.

He's standing on a tattered throw rug.

He has his arms stretched out.

He says that he wants a hug.

There's a man in an old Chevy.

He's smoking a long straight-necked pipe.

There's a man in my room standing in the dark.

There's a man all alone out in the street tonight.

He has his hand on my shoulder.

He says everything will be all right.

There's a man on a stool.

He can't get up.

There's a man on his knees.

But he won't say please.

There's a man at a bar with his foot on the rail.

There's a man on a porch.

He looks like he's angry.

There's a man in my life.

He thinks he's my dad.

There's a man pacing the kitchen with a pain in his chest.

There's a man on a bed and his face is all white.

There's a man in a box and his cheeks are all rosy.

His hair is black and wavy.

His eyes are shut up tight.

I reached out to touch the back of his hand.

It looked quite red.

It was cold.

It was lifeless.

The man in the box was dead.

MISTER DUCHNOWSKI'S BEAN SUPPERS

The majority of my friends, and myself, spent the most of our young adult lives ... looking for love in all of the wrong places. I don't think that we knew what we were doing. I don't think that we realized that we were looking for love. But that is what we were doing. That is what we are all doing ... no matter how we express or try to deny it. That is what we are doing.

Mister Duchnowski was the dad of one of my bosom lifelong buddies. Every time that we saw him, he had the same advice for us. We had heard his advice so many times, that we knew his lecture by heart. We were always respectful to Mister D., but for the most part we thought of him as somewhat odd. I think that he knew what we thought, but he continued to give us the same speech nevertheless. There were times when we just laughed. We never took him seriously. We never really listened to his well intended lecture. And, we never followed his advice.

Today, Mister Duchnowski is no longer with us, but I can still see him smiling, his teeth back home on the bureau soaking in a glass, his stained, flat-topped golf cap stationed askew atop his wavy gray, and those Polish eyes sparkling sincerely and hopefully as he offered to us his best thought considerations with regards to our future love life. I still smile as I hear his voice, but now that I am the age that he was then, I have to think twice about what he was trying to say to us. I don't think that we should have been laughing.

Here's to you Mister D; and here's Mister D to the all of you.

MR. DUCHNOWSKI'S BEAN SUPPERS

Listen to me ... listen to me!
You guys is entirely on the wrong track, ya see.

Skip the nightclubs, the booze, and the dim lights.
Take yourself down to a church bean supper one of these
      nights.

The prettiest girls that you have ever seen,
Are right there in the line, spoonin' out the beans.

I know, I know, you think that I'm old and outta my mind,
But believe me, at them ham and bean suppers
Are the prettiest girls that you'll ever find.

You wouldn't believe the girl last night
Slicin' up the German rye.
It gave ten years back to my life
Just to see that sweet look in her eye.

And next to her, with the Polish Kielbasey,
Was an Italian girl by the name of Bonacarsee.

That dark hair and olive skin ... she could a been a movie star.
And there you guys are, down some dive or two bit bar.

What do you think you're gonna meet down there?
You guys are missin' it, I'm tellin' ya ... but I don't care.

My life's over. It's no matter to me.
But if it's beautiful girls that you're lookin' for
Them bean suppers is where you oughta be.
That's right! That's right!

Oh yeah, you can laugh all you want,
But them church bean suppers
Are the places you guys oughta haunt.
The prettiest girls that I've ever seen,
Spoonin' out pork 'n beans like outta some dream.

You guys is just missin' the boat.
Why it puts a lump right here in my throat
To think if I was you guy-es age,
I'll tell ya, I wouldn't be watchin' some nude-y
Dancin' in some cage.

I'd be down to one of them bean suppers, in a rush
Tryin' to steal a smile or pinch a blush
From one of them lovelies with sauce on her apron,
And bread flour smearin' her chest.

Take it from me, it's at them bean suppers
Where the girls are the best.

You can leave it behind ... you can forget all the rest,
Try one of them church bean suppers

And then you tell me if them girls ain't the best.
That's right! That's right!
You try one of them bean suppers some night.
Then you come back and tell me if old Mr. Duchnowski
Didn't tell ya what's right.

You just try one of them bean suppers some night
And see if what I tell you ain't right.

WALTER

Walter owned "Walter's Variety" on Exchange St. in the old neighborhood. Walter was a tough talking, warm hearted local entrepreneur who was kind enough to provide us little neighborhood guys a sanctuary on those cold, New England, winter evenings.

We sat in a little cubbyhole reading comic books, drinking hot chocolate or "tonic" and eating nickel bags of Granite State potato chips.

Dobson was a wild little guy who at a very early age managed to "borrow" his mother's car periodically. He lived at the top of Exchange St. and would come racing down the hill. He would stop on the corner of Exchange and Center Streets at Walter's Variety, rev up his engine and then peel, screech, slip and slide across the street.

Whenever Walter heard that screeching sound he would burst into the following admonition.

ON A SLAB

On a slab!
That S.O.B. is gonna be on a slab.

They won't need no autopsy or blood work at the lab.
They'll just scrape the pieces up
And spread that sucker out on a slab.

You kids will never learn.
You think that you're so smart.
You think that you know it all.

Well, go ahead, race around like a bunch of nuts.
Prove to the world that you've got the guts.

Then it's down the morgue ... on a slab!
That's where you're gonna end up, my boys ... on a slab!

I'll come and visit you down the morgue...
"Hullo, is that my friend Dobson in vault 101, 102 ... and 104?
A little piece here,
A little piece there...
Here's a piece of skull
With some of that wavy black hair.

No blood test down the lab,
It's Mr. Dobson ... on a slab!

He'll be on a slab!
That S.O.B., he'll be on a slab!

Then his mother will be over cryin' to me.
"Oh, he was such a good little boy.
He just thought that an automobile was a toy."

On a slab!
My little friend is gonna be ... on a slab!

They won't need no blood test down the lab.
They'll just scrape that little sucker up,

And spread him out on slab!

Like jam and peanut butter down at the lab,
They'll just spread our pal Dobson out...
On a slab!

AND THE RIVER FLOWS

A child is standing behind a closed, abandoned, department store that backs up to the Spicket River.

He tries to toss broken chips of concrete from his side of the river over to the other.

He tries to hit and break discarded soda bottles lying along the opposite bank.

A man is watching the boy from the second storey window of the textile mill.

He's smoking a cigarette.

He's on his break.

Beneath him the purple water from the textile mill dye, tumbles from a giant pipe.

It tumbles from the pipe and it foams and bubbles, as it splashes into the river below.

It forms a purple, yellow, greenish cloud of bubbling foam on the surface of the river,

And it floats off down stream, a patchwork of multi-colored bubbles.

A scalloped damn has been formed from floating debris,

And they both watch as a discarded box-spring is freed from the back and into the river's flow.

The river is shallow.

It flows around exposed rocks and rubble and rubber tires ... and truck axles ... and rusted, metal bicycle rims.

There are boards, and sticks, and parts of fallen trees.

The box spring gets hung up on a boulder, and a partially submerged stump.

The boy rushes around the bank.

He picks up a long, somewhat bent piece of iron pipe.

He walks out onto the river,

Stepping from one pile of hung up debris to the next, until finally he reaches the box-spring.

He pries at it with his piece of pipe.

He pushes and shoves, he wants to set it free.

He wants to see it roll with the current,

And rush along with the river.

He has one foot on a huge, soggy cardboard box,

And the other on a two foot splinter of broken plywood.

He almost has the box spring free.

He pushes and stretches with his pipe.

One last shove ... oomph! ... and it's free!

But the boy tumbles into the rushing water.

He screams! ... He fumbles and rolls onto his back.

The man on his break throws the window up.

He whistles through his fingers ... then yells!

"Stand up, kid! ... STAND UP!"

The boy hears the man.

He rolls and scrambles to his feet.

The water rushes between his legs.

It is not deep enough to rise above his knees.

He feels dumb.

He was really scared.

He thought that he was going to drown.

He looks up at the man in the window and smiles.

His smile has a tooth missing on one side,

And one of his front teeth is chipped.

The man in the window shakes his head,

And flips his cigarette out and into the quiet, gray wind.

It tumbles and tosses in the air.

Then it rolls, lightly, onto the river top, and immediately it dances off

With the splashing twisting current.

The boy watches the river rush between his legs.

It plasters his pants to his shins.

He forms the palms of his hands into a cup,

And dips them into the stream.

He lifts the water up, and splashes it onto his face.

"Hey! ... What are you nuts?" the man from the mill window yells.

"Don't put that onto your face. Get the hell out of that river and go home."

The boy looks up at the man. He cups his hands again

And dips them back into the water.

He lifts them to his face.

He slurps the water up and into his mouth.

Then he squirts it out between his lips.

He spits it up towards the man in the mill window.

When the boy finishes spitting the water up at the man, he grins.

The man shakes his head, disapprovingly,

Then waves his fist at the boy.

The boy scoops up more water...

Slurps it into his mouth, and again,

Spits it towards the man in the window.

"Go ahead, drink it. Kill yourself.

It would be good enough for you. Drink it! I dare ya, drink it."

The boy bends at the waist, and scoops up more water.

He stops momentarily.

The boy drops the water and laughs.

"What's the matter ... you chicken? ... Drink it ... Drink it!"

And the man bends

And braces himself on the window sill,

Then shoves his head out the window and laughs.

The boy stares up at the man.

"What? Do you think I'm stupid?" he yells.

"You look pretty stupid to me," the man yells back.

"Oh yeah?"

"Yeah!"

"Well, I might be stupid,

But I'm not dumb enough to work in that stinkin' mill."

The man stares down at the boy. He pauses;

Shakes his head in disgust;

Then draws himself back inside

And slams the window shut.

From the inside he continues to stare down at the boy

Through the dust and dirt-stained window pane.

And the river flows

And so ... and so

The river flows.

A CHILD OF NIGHT

The rain rushes and sparkles in streaks
Past the bright, white streetlight globe.
Within its light, all is bright, and knowing and clean.
But beyond its gleam, all is dead, and black and red,
And nothing is what it seems.

It wouldn't be so bad, and he wouldn't be so sad,
If it weren't for the night and the fright of the Devil by night.
Beyond every crack, and below every track,
It's the Devil, THE DEVIL! The Devil … He's back.
And God doesn't care because
He's combing His hair and fixing His gowns,
And counting the jewels that the angels have found.
So what can be done, but to run and to run, to cry and to
        scream
And to hide in the light of each streetlight beam.

If he had a friend, or maybe a dog,
Who would bark and would bite,
And maybe grab onto the tail of the Devil by night;
And fight, and bite, and grab onto the tail of the Devil by
        night,
He could make his way from beam to beam,
And run in the shade that the rain drops made,
And get to the bakery for the bread and the buns,
And the rolls with the creams,
And escape the evil of his devilish dreams.

But instead, he would have to go it alone and deal with the
dead
And the black and the red
And the bodies of all those who have ever been dead.

He longed as he ran and leaped from fright
Over cracks and potholes in the street that night,
To see the ovens and the heat and the glow from the baker's
light;
Like a halo at night, shining bright,
What a wondrous sight all powdery white,
With sugars and creams
And all the love and warmth of the streetlight beams.

Under his jacket, he would put his bread,
And with his hat he'd cover his head.
Then off he would go, into the rain and the snow
Pushing and shoving for that streetlight glow,
And when he'd get home, he'd be safe and sound,
And all the Devils would be back in the ground,
And the cracks and the trees, and the shadows and the breeze,
And the rain and the fright,
And the hooting owls of night,
And the tears and the cold,
And the demons so bold,
With their braces of gold,
And their teeth of mold,
And the gurgling pipes,
And the sewers and snipes,
And the black and the red,
And all that's been dead,

And the buildings that sway,
And the noises that prey,
And the shadows that grow,
And the heels that click,
And the boots that clomp,
And the doors that bang,
And the signs that rattle,
And the night that fights against all that is right
Will be gone.

And he'll be home and ready for bed.
And dear God, he'll say, I made this day,
And I hope you'll remember, the tears and the fears
And the years upon years, that you howled in my ears,
And that you won't delight,
In the ghoul and the horror and the evil of might
To take pleasure in the tears and the fright of a child of night.

HUMOR

UNDER THE INFLUENCE

"This dog-gone country is goin' to the dogs!
All they can ever think of
Is makin' a whole bunch a more laws!"
Then old Russell took a swig on his beer, for a pause.

"Yup, it's just goin' downhill ... goin' to the dogs!
Take this drunken drivin' and all these darn new laws.
Why a fella can't even have a drink,
Before some cop is on top a him with one of them claws.

"I mean, there I am...
They took away my license last year..."
Then old Russell took another slug of beer.

"I'm tryin' to get home
Goin' down one of them dark back roads
When all of a sudden,
One of them unmarked cars with the sirens unloads.
Jerked my heart ... nearly sent me into a ditch;
That gosh darn foolhardy son of a switch!

"I'll tell ya, I think a man drives better when he's drunk.
He drives more careful, I mean, gosh-darn,
A man knows he's drunk when he's drunk!
He don't race around slippin' and slidin'.
Heck, he's got all he can do to keep from collidin'.

"I mean drivin' drunk makes a man nervous enough,
Tryin' to keep a straight line and all that stuff.
Why, when I'm drivin' drunk, so's I can barely see
The last thing that I need
Is some darn cop hidin' behind some tree!

"Why, I'll tell you the truth;
It's them sneekin' Po-leece that's the problem for us all.
Get rid of them sons-a-guns,
And we'll get this country's horse out of this stall!"

THE CALL OF THE WILD

Yes, I've answered to the call of the wild,
And traveled to some far off places.

I've slept in the loft, and under that bridge,
And stared at some mighty strange faces.

I've heard the geese, and the wild turkeys clatter,
And a number of meals I've missed,
But now that's hardly a matter.

And it was truly wondrous to lay on the pine straw
And sleep with the stars over head.

But all in all, my friends, there is a lot to be said
For a big fluffy pillow and a factory made bed.

It doesn't have to be the Serta Perfect Sleeper.
The less well known does a pretty good job,
And it's a heck of a lot cheaper.

I've washed my hair in a babbling brook
And bathed naked in a cold mountain stream.

I've sipped water as it tumbled
And foamed through jagged rocks,
And tramped on tankers to worldly docks.

I've sat by the campfire and listened to old yarns,
And more than once made love out behind that old barn.

And it sure is nice to stare into that log fire
With the stars twinkling over head.
But by the bye, I'll skip that sky,
For a big fluffy pillow and a factory made bed.

Ah yes, I was young and remember the days
When I laughed at the notion of changing my ways.

When all of the girls were so darn pretty,
And I couldn't get enough of them bars or that City.

There was poker and smoke and plenty of gin.
You could bob my noggin' and raise nothin' but a grin.

Those were the days; I'll tell ya my friend.
Drop my head on a curb of granite
And dream a dream of Carol or Janet.

But now that noodle is more like strudel,
And when I flop down this weary old head,

It had best hit onto a big fluffy pillow
Lying on top of a factory made bed.

I NEED ANOTHER POOR FOLK SONG

I need another poor folk song.
One filled with butter beans and turnip greens.
Got a condo in El Paso
From singin' 'bout my lasso.

I'm a big country singer.
My gal-friend's a real ring-dinger.
I've got a chain of restaurants that makes a million,
Grillin' chitterlings fer yer chill-ren.

But I need another poor folk song
Or my fans will forget me afore too long.
I'd like one that talks about bar-b-que
Black-eyed peas and how'd-ya-do.

I've worn out all my pick-em-up trucks
And 'Tractor Trailers'... made big bucks.
But now I need another poor folk song
Or my fans will forget me afore too long.

I need one dealin' with say, leather, and filigree
With a good refrain and a tweedle-dee-dee
Don't know how I'd like it to begin
But I'll sing it with pathos and a cowboy grin.

I'd like one that could bring a tear to your eye.
Make even your spoiled rotten little brother cry.

I need me another poor folk song
Before I get a hitch in my get-a-long.

I've got fourteen accountants, old pard,
And a genuine full sized replica of the B&O Railroad in my
        back yard.
I've had eleven dee-vorces
And my own race track, complete with horses.

I own the San Diego Padres
And the San Antonio Madres
I bought four professional basketball teams
And I'm runnin' out of stupid things to buy even in my dreams.

But if I don't get me another poor folk song
My fans will forget me afore too long.
I made it big with that one about the chewin' gum.
Hit the top ten with ... "Cow-Bum Dung"

Made ten million on "Spittin' and Chewin'"
But now dang it, I need a new-un.
I need me another poor folk song.
Or my fans will forget me afore too long.

Yessiree,
        ... I need me another poor folk song.

GRANDMA'S COMING

Grandma's coming!
Let's clean all the pots, and boil all the pans,
Wash all the tots, and scrub all their hands.

I hope, in the plates, we can all see our face,
Because ...you know how Mother hates, dirt and dust all over
   the place.

Clean up the shed, and pick up the toys,
Make up the bed, and warn the boys...

Grandma's coming, so do what you're told.
No chewing gum, or guitar strumming,
You know, your ma's mother's coming.

Let's make this house fit for a king.
We'll use the good silver and every fine thing.

Let's clean out the oven, which hasn't been cleaned,
Since Eleanor Roosevelt's mother was weaned.

Tell all the neighbors, we ain't gonna sell.
It's just Grandma, visiting for a spell.

There's only one thing that ruffles my fur,
If all year, this old place is good enough for me...

WHY THE HECK AIN'T IT GOOD ENOUGH FOR HER!

BARROOM BUDDIES

"Jerry, ah ... I don't say things like this too often...
Hey Ernie! Another round over here...
Now, where was I?"

"You don't say things like this too often..."

"Oh yeah! Well I'm not the kind of guy
Who forgets things.
I appreciate you, my friend.
Put' er there. I mean it, Buddy.
I wanna shake your hand.
A guy don't have too many real friends in this life,
And you are one, pal. I mean it...

"Hey, talk about real friends!
Look across the bar over there.
You see that guy all dressed up in that fancy suit?
That man and I have really been through some times together.
I mean, I grew up with that guy.
We lived on the same street.
I've known that guy since we were this high.
I mean, I knew him when he didn't have a nickel.
And look at him now! Dressed to kill!
He must of hit the jackpot.
And I'll bet he don't even recognize me.
I mean, I haven't seen him
Since we got out of the Service together.
HEY, you old rascal! Where the hell you been?

Look at you! You look like a million bucks."

"Hey, don't I wish. Don't let these duds fool you.
I'm about as flat as a pancake.
Lost every damn cent I ever had.
I'm wearin' this suit because it's all I got left.
I mean things have gone really sour for me, Bob.
I'll tell you how bad it really is.
I don't even have enough money to buy another drink.
You wouldn't buy an old fightin' buddy a drink,
Would ya Bob?
I'd really appreciate it.
You just don't know how thirsty a guy can get, old friend.
It's like a desert out here."

"Ah, gee Georgie, I really wish I could, but I'm flat broke..."
[Bob leaned forward, and with his elbows,
covered the bills and change lying in front of him on the bar.]

"Oh come on, Bob ... for old time sake?
We were two of a kind, we two.
Just one for old time sake?
And I swear to god, I won't bother you again."

"I really wish I could, pal, but I'm out ... flat out, buddy."
[Bob's well dressed friend across the bar, raises from his stool,
shakes his head in anguish at the floor, then heads for the
barroom door.]

"I thought he was you're old time friend?
Your bosom Buddy?

48

Your best pal? You went through thick and thin together?
Old army buddies ... Lived on the same street? ...
Never forget the time you and he did so and so?"

"That's true."

"And you wouldn't even buy the poor slob a drink?"

"Hey, he'll find another sucker...
Besides, once a drunk, always a drunk...
You know what I mean?"

BIG JIM

Big Jim was his name and plumbing his game.
When it came to a leak, a pipe or brass fixture,
He was the man with the torch and lead mixture.
There wasn't a joint that Big Jim couldn't sweat,
Be it horizontal or vertical.
He knew his stuff, you bet,
When it came to things metallurgical.

But I say with a sigh, and this no lie,
Our Big Jim was a Mr. Five by Five.
And as he grew older,
His waist far surpassed his broad shoulder.
He was quite a guy, Big Jim Sheehy, Mr. Five by Five.

One night when Big Jim was on his way home
From Cain and Bernard's,
He stumbled into a cruiser
That had jumped in the path to his yard.

By way of explanation,
Big Jim began to recite, in expletive,
The American Declaration.
Then, with intention beguiling,
He burst into stanza ...
The theme from Bonanza
And a chorus or two of 'When Irish Eyes Are Smiling.'

Big Jim thought it quite appropriate,
But the cops thought that he should go to-the-poke-for-it.
So one by one, they leapt from the cruiser,
Thinking that they would subdue the five by five bruiser.

They wailed with their clubs and grabbed for his thumbs,
While Big Jim just laughed and dropped to his buns.
"I give, I give ... I'm a peaceable fellow,"
Big Jim, from the ground, he did bellow.

"Well you're disturbin' the peace, and we're the police,
And we're here to entail
And cart your butt down to the jail."

"Well you go right ahead, and I'd never resist,
But I'm afraid I'm too tipsy to help or assist."

So with effort of perspiration and sweat,
It was something to see,
As deputies Pee and Wee
Struggled 'till soaking wet.

They swore and they cussed,
As they tumbled and fussed
And tugged at Big Jim's anchor.
But he was broad a' beam
And jellyroll mean,
And too laughable to cause any rancor.

So they gave him a stay, as on the ground he lay,
Then wagged their fingers in warnin'.

"We're gonna let ya go,
Though you darn well know,
That we're the police
And you're disturbin' the peace,
One wise peep and we'll be back with recruits,
Pulleys and shoots
And cart ya off to the jail house in the mornin'."

MURDER

Little Danny took his blows,
As he stood against a bigger, toe to toe.

A right, a left, a blow to the gut,
And Danny was down again dustin' his butt.

I had never seen a fight like this,
As freckled faced Danny put up his fists.

Knocked down, and bowled over,
He got knuckled from shoulder to shoulder.

But Danny took it blow for blow,
And stood his ground, toe to toe.

I had never seen a boy get beaten so badly,
It was Danny Mulroon, and Robert Bradley.

Robert had the height, the reach and the jab,
He had the walk, the talk, and the gift for the gab.

"You'd best stay where y'er at, Danny Mulroon,
'cause I'm gonna knock ya bloody from now 'till noon.
I've already beaten a lot bigger than you,
I just give 'em a taste of me old one-two."

Robert had hands as quick as his feet,
And Danny was a boy who was sorely beat.

But, up he'd leap from off the ground,
Only to get tumbled and pummeled and knocked again down.

He was a bloody mess, that Danny Mulroon.
If he kept gettin' up he'd be dead before noon.

Robert's fists kept crackin' his face,
To stand and watch was even a disgrace.

Each time he'd tumble, even the ground would moan.
It was too much of a beatin' for a boy half grown.

"Give it up Danny.
Give it up, son.
We know ya got courage.
Now let it be done."

But Danny would stumble again to his feet,
And Bobby would slam him like a piece of dead meat.

Some of the crowd began to walk away.
It was a loss, but Danny just wouldn't give way.

It went on and on 'till the crowd had all left,
As Bobby showed Danny who was the best.

Danny's eyes were closed swollen, his nose a red glow,
His lips both broken, his jaw hangin' low.

"I'm tellin' ya to stay down," said Bobby Bradley,
With a hint of a tear and a voice that cracked sadly.

But when Danny heard that slight sigh of regret,
He knew that his fight was not over yet.

He leapt from the ground and rushed to his foe,
And Bobby just crumbled from his head to his toe.

He fell to the ground like a sack of sweat.
I can hear his cryin' and wailin' still yet.

Danny never hit Bobby a blow,
But there was Bobby on the ground below.

"Get up and fight like a man!" cried Danny,
Standing up straight like a tiny Vic Tanny.

A sight like this I had never seen.
The boy on the ground was neat and clean.

The boy who was beat and bleeding defeat,
Was tellin' the victor to get up on his feet.

"If you've had enough, then say ya give..!"

"I give ... I give ..." said Bobby Bradley,
"You win, I give ... I tell ya I give.
My mother would kill me.
It would really hurt her,
If her only son should go to jail for murder."

WAY BACK WHEN

You should have known me way back when.
I was really somethin' then.

You would have liked me years ago,
When I was just a regular Joe.

Back then with all my friends and pals,
When boys were guys and girls were gals.

You would have really liked me then,
In my good old days, way back when.

In those days, I was always bustin' with a smile,
And laughin' and jokin' all the while.

You would have liked me way back then,
Before I turned old and God wrinkled my skin.

Before my laugh burnt out, the wages of sin,
And my grin perspired at the bottom of a bottle of gin.

You would have liked me way back when.
Yup, I was really somethin' then.

I loved to work and break a brow.
Spent a year, one day, behind a plow.

I loved to rove and wander down under.
I spat at the rain and laughed at its thunder.

I was really somethin' way back when.
You would have liked me, if you knew me then.

Never pestered a cat or kicked a dog,
Before I got hooked on the mug and the grog.

Never cussed or bucked at the load.
Never complained I had too much to tow.

Yes Sir, I was quite a guy, way back when.
You all would have liked me, if you knew me then.

I wasn't all grumpy and pestered with pain.
Believe it or not, women even kissed me before age made me
        tame.
I used to empty my pockets and throw away the change.
I even bucked a bronco once and roamed on a range.

I was really somethin' way back when.
You would have really liked me then.

I wasn't always this ugly and bent at the back.
When I was young there was no where that this old man went
        slack.
I was quite a guy and lots of fun,
Way back in them good old days when I was young.

So when you look at me now and think what a shame.
Remember if you live long enough, you'll look much the same.

You won't be as spry and as quick with a joke.
You'll think yourself lucky to be one of us older folk.

Yes indeed, I was quite a guy, way back when,
And you might not believe it, but you would have liked me
    then.
Yup, I was really somethin' way back when.
And you really would have liked me, if you knew me then.

WORK TO DO

I think that this next poem is not only my story, but the story of the most of us. After all, there is only so much room at the top of the pile. And, there would hardly be a top, if there were no pile to begin with.

It is said that God must have truly loved the poor or He wouldn't have made so many of them. Clearly, He must have felt much the same with regards to dreamers.

WORK TO DO

You know ... you know,
I think I could be an astronaut.

I know I could! BLAST OFF! Ground Zero...
One small step for man - one giant step for mankind...

I could do better than that. I know I could! I'm sure!
I'm sure that I have the right stuff.

"Yeah right! But for now, my lad,
Take hold of this line and tow the mark.
We've got a week of work to do
Before this day turns dark."

You know ... you know,
I I I bet I could be a playwright!

I know I could!

Exit, stage left.
Enter, stage right ... pst, pst (aside)...
Opening nights, tuxedos, beautiful gowns...
"Alas, poor Horatio, I knew him well."

Boy, if I just had the chance. I could do it.
I KNOW I COULD!

"Ah huh! But for now, my boy,
Let's sweep the lobby and clean the commode.
We got a storeroom to clean,
And a truck to unload.
So take hold of this line and tow the mark.
We've got a week of work to do
Before this day turns dark."

You know ... You know ...
I'm sure that I could have been a great chef.
One of them tall hats and a pile of crepes,
Chocolate mousse, fancy wine?
I could have made the shop where the wealthy dine.

"No doubt, sugar!
But this burger needs more fire
And the boss just put a sign on the door that says...
COOK FOR HIRE.
So take hold of this line
And tow the mark.
We got a week of work to do
Before this day turns dark."

You know, you know,
I could have been one of those guys
Who builds scrapers in the sky,
Or bridges in the air, or rockets out in space!
I know that I could Frank-Lloyd-Wright with all my might.

"I'm sure you could.
But right now we gotta lay eight hundred more block
And we ain't even on the clock.
So grab hold of this line
And tow the mark.
We've got a week of work to do
Before this day turns dark."

Grab hold of the line, poor boy,
And tow the mark.
You've got a lifetime of work to do
Before this day turns dark.

NOBODY LIKES YOU

I am going to take this onto myself,
Simply because no one else seems to be willing to do it.

I feel that you should know and be made to understand.
No one should be allowed to live in a complete delusion.

Now you listen to me.
PUT DOWN THAT NEWSPAPER!

Are you listening?
"Yes, I am."

Okay -
No ... one ... likes ... you!
Let me repeat that,
Just in case you weren't paying attention.

Look at me now! Okay, let me repeat
NO ... ONE ... LIKES ... YOU!

Did you get that?
Now I'm telling it to you like it is.

Absolutely no one who knows you,
Intimately or otherwise, cares for you one iota.

Your mother ... that's right!
Your mother told me before she died,

That you were nothing but a pompous ass.

You are not constantly being disconnected
By a faulty line at the phone company.

Those people are hanging up on you.
You are abusive.

You are old and you are abusive.
Your employees all think that you are a skinflint.

You are so cheep you make Jack Benny
Look like a big spender.

You pay out wages to people as if
They are being donated to a charitable organization.

Let me clue you in,
Your employees think that they more than earn
The pittance that they are begrudgingly granted
By Your Highness.

You live like a coolie;
And you are loaded.
What in God's name is wrong with you?

Don't tell me about the damn Depression.
I'm as old as you are and I know darn well
You weren't even alive during the Depression.

You were born in an age of prosperity.

Your parents were professionals.
You are simply ... cheap.

You are so cheap you reek.
You are small minded.
You are jealous of everybody.
You think you know everything.
You are an elitist, obnoxious, pompous ass.

If you didn't have the money
To pay for other people's attention,
There is nobody in this world
Who would even talk to you.

"I feel that you are exaggerating."

I could have guessed.

IF I WERE A BUTTERFLY

If I were a butterfly,
I could flap my wings,
And fly from flower to flower...
Hour ... upon hour ... upon hour.

But if I were a butterfly,
I wouldn't fly too high,
For I could get caught
In the wind currents high in the sky.
And I wouldn't fly over the ocean,
For I'd never be able to rest.
If I sat in the water
My wings would get wet.

But oh, how wondrous it would be,
To fly from flower to flower,
Hour ... upon hour ... upon hour.

But if I were a butterfly,
I couldn't hop or skip or jump.
I couldn't eat homemade soup
Or potato pancakes
With sour cream for my lunch.
I couldn't sit in an easy chair by a log fire.
Or crawl into a warm bed when I want to retire.

BUT, IF I WERE A BUTTERFLY,
I COULD FLY

From flower ... to flower?
Hour ... upon hour ... upon hour?

But I couldn't drink, or think,
Or talk with my friends,
Or hold hands, and walk in the park,
Or stay up all night and sit in the dark.
I couldn't sing or dance or play,
Or dream about a better day.
I couldn't hope ... or care, or want, or dare...

BUT I COULD FLY!
YES, I COULD FLY!
AND I COULD FLY FROM FLOWER TO FLOWER.
YES, AND I COULD FLY
FROM FLOWER TO FLOWER...
HOUR ... UPON HOUR ... UPON HOUR.

YES, YES! I could fly from flower to flower,
Hour ... upon hour ... upon hour!
Upon hour ... upon hour ... upon hour?

I COULD FLY ... I COULD FLY!

And then end up on the side of a road to die?
Or in a collector's net?
Or pressed between the pages of a book?
Or under a microscope for someone to take a look?

I'd be so lovely and so free
Everyone would want to get a hold of me.

Yes, if I were a butterfly, I could fly,
But I couldn't sigh or cry ... or even tell a lie.
If I were a butterfly,
Could a falling raindrop break my neck?

Oh, what the heck...

MAYBE I COULD BE A BIRD!

NO, HE IS NOT LIKE HE USED TO BE

No he is not exactly like he used to be.
He often sits on the porch and stares vacantly
As the cars pass by.

Sometimes he appears to be confused
Over the slightest interruption
To his daily routine.

He complains more than he ever had.
Now he seems to whine constantly
About nothing in particular.

His hair is always looking rough.
And he seems to be losing a bit of it
More and more each day.

His appetite is good.
We can't seem to stop him from nibbling
And poking at something.

He eats far too much chocolate.
He never used to eat cookies,
And the ice cream is getting out of hand.

He seems to be limping
A little bit lately.
And he has been stumbling.

He is not hearing well.
It is rather obvious.
You have to talk right at him.

He probably isn't seeing all that well either.
But he hates going to see a Doctor
Or a specialist of any kind.

The old boy is getting old.
He just ain't what he used to be.
But I love him so.

He has always been so good to me.
He always did his best to make me happy.
I can't really fault him for anything.

But this old age is a hard thing to deal with.
No more solo flights for this guy.
I've really got to watch him.

Especially when he tries to climb the cedar tree
Next to the house
And get up onto the roof.

OVER AND OVER

I say the same thing over.
I say it over and over.
I say the same thing over;
Over and over, and over.

I say the same thing over.
I'm a lover, a rover, a drover.
I say the same thing over;
Over, and over, and over.

I say the same thing over.
Sometimes I say "moreover,"
But I say the same thing over and over;
Over and over, and over.

I say the same thing over.
I grow older, and older, and older,
But I say the same thing over and over;
Over, and over, and over.

I say the same thing over.
I say it as I grow older and older.
But, now, let me say "moreover,"
Because I'm getting tired of saying the same thing,
Over, and over, and over.

I say the same thing over.
I say it over and over.

I say it now bolder and bolder.
But, I say it over and over;
Over, and over, and over.

I say it with a glance over my shoulder.
I say it peeking from behind a huge boulder.
But, I say the same thing over and over;
Over, and over, and over.

But, in conclusion, I would like to say "moreover,"
Because, as you know, I have now said
The same thing over and over;
Over, and over, and over.

I've said it from behind my back,
And over my shoulder.
But, I've said the same thing over and over;
Over, and over, and over.

You don't notice it, I suppose,
Because sometimes I say "moreover,"
But, really, I assure you, I'm saying the same thing
Over and over;
Over, and over, and over.

If you go back to the beginning
And read what I've said ... over,
You will find that I have said the same thing
Over, and over;
Over, and over, and over.

Occasionally, I've said "moreover,"
But from the beginning to the end,
I wouldn't lie, my friend,
I've said the same thing over and over;
Over, and over, and over.

I've said it when younger, and when older.
I've said it from behind my back and over my shoulder.
I've said it while peeking from behind a huge boulder,
But, believe it or not, I've said the same thing
Over and over;
Over, and over, and over.

LOVE AND OTHER NICE THINGS

MY LITTLE FRIEND

When I was little, I had a friend.

We said that we would be friends,

    ... until the end.

We didn't lie.

And when he died,

    ... I cried and I cried

        ... and I cried.

A CHRISTMAS CAROL

Carol is a pleasant rhyme,
Enjoying, laughing, Christmas time
Snow filled streets and trees alike,
Bows and tinsel, a shinny red bike.

Those crisp, clean, nights.
The stars, what a sight!
Sleigh bells ringing, a child's delight.
It brings one's heart to a new found height.

Carol is a pleasant rhyme,
Enjoying, laughing, Christmas time.
The smell of outdoors, a pine tree bristles
Puppy dogs, bright red berries, boughs and thistles.

Hands in mittens, a pretty white kitten,
Cupid abounds with hearts all smitten,
A poppin' fire, a reindeer for hire,
A mysterious box full of switches and brier.

Carol is a pleasant rhyme,
Singing, laughing, Christmas time.
Boys in love, and girls all a glow
Silent whispers and stolen kisses beneath mistletoe.

Bonnets and babies, sweet memories so old,
Hopes for the future and good things to hold,
Keepsakes, and sonnets, a locket of gold,
Those times of youth, so daring and bold.

Carol is a pleasant rhyme,
Enjoying laughing Christmas time,
Cherries and chocolate and ice cream balls,
Dancing and singing and decking the halls.

Carol is a pleasant rhyme.
Carol is for Christmas time.
Carol is all things in time.
Carol is a love of mine.

SOMETIMES I SEE HIM, BUT THEN HE'S GONE

We go through life blind. We see only momentarily, through the eyes of art, love, or knowledge. They awaken vision with a start. Suddenly we see for the first time a mailbox, or a Campbell's tomato soup can. And when we do, we are shocked that we have never seen this thing before. Why? What have we been doing that is so important that we have never noticed these things before? Where have we been, that we have never noticed until this moment, the beautiful sparkle of the sun's light skimming across the bay at mid afternoon. Where have we been that we have never felt before, this tingle of warmth that prickles our skin as we sit on this sandy beach? What has occupied us to this point of numbness where we don't even see joy in one another, where beautiful things and people pass unnoticed, where even those who are most dear to us slip our attention, where laughter and tears draw from us only contempt? Where have we been? What are we doing? Why is life being wasted on us? Why do I only see her or him at those moments of need? Why do I only appreciate the values of kindness and compassion when they are being shown to me, and feel nothing but cynicism when they are demanded of me? And when I see you, at those rare moments, with open eyes of love ... do you ever see me?

This is another one of many poems that has been inspired by my wife. At times she would capture me at the kitchen, or while I was shaving in the bathroom. She would brush back my hair, or rub her hand along my cheek to see if I hand done a good job with my razor. All the while she would be staring into my eyes. The only other person in this life who ever looked at me in such a way was my Grandmother. I could never stay away from my Grandmother. I knew what that look meant.

At these moments when my wife would stare at me, with this sparkle of grinning warmth, I would always question how many times had I looked at her in such a way? Far too few, I'm afraid ... far too few.

SOMETIMES I SEE HIM, BUT THEN HE'S GONE

I see him when I hold him in my arms, but then he's gone.

I see him when he's hungry for my charms, but then he's gone.

I see him sometimes when he looks into my eyes, when it's

    morning,

Or it's evening, or when he's hiding from all the lies.

I see him sometimes, but then he's gone.

I see him hiding from the crowd, but then he's gone.

I know he needs me, but he will never tell me.

He's much too proud, and often times too loud.

Sometimes when I see my reflection in his eyes,

My knees turn to jelly, and my cries turn to sighs.

But then it's over ... and he's gone.

A moment, a flash, a little twinkle,

I see him ... but then he's gone.

And I know him, and I see him, and I love him,

But sometimes I wonder?

       ... Does he ever see me?

SHE CAME TO SEE ME

I once owned a little ice cream parlor on the outskirts of a small town. Many of my customers were older people who lived in a retirement village up the road. It was hard to build a business in this atmosphere - as fast as I gained new customers, I lost an old one to ... time.

The old folks always came in couples, until one day, one of the two would stumble in, awkwardly ... alone. It was difficult to know the right thing to say. You didn't want to say; Hey, where's Rita or Bob? Because if you did, out would come the handkerchief and down the wrinkled cheeks would flow the tears. So if the remaining party didn't say anything, you didn't say anything.

Often times nothing would be said. Sometimes there would be a brief announcement that there was no more Herb, or Ethel. Then with others there would be a long involved explanation of the last weeks or months or year.

When I was a young person, I didn't want to hear such stories. As an older person I no longer had that problem. These were all beautiful stories, filled with love. These were all stories about people who cared about one another. They were sad, but...

On one occasion this very sad, and very alone, old man came into the shop. He had been in a few times now, without his chum. He had gotten his hot fudge, caramel brownie sundae and had left without saying anything. On this particular occasion, though, he was smiling and seemed relieved. He told me a story that I have converted into a small poem and I entitled it:

SHE CAME TO SEE ME

I saw you in my dream last night.
You seemed to be so happy where you were.
You were laughing once again.

You were frightened when you left.
You wept,
And clasped my hand.

You didn't know where you were going.
I saw the fear in your eyes.
I saw the tears.

But last night in my dream
You were laughing again.
You were, once again, yourself.

Last night you were telling your jokes.
You smiled.
You were happy and relieved.

Thank-you for coming to see me.
You looked so pretty, my dear.
You were so rosy, my lovely friend.

I feel so much better knowing that you're safe.
Now I won't worry anymore.
Thank-you my dear.

Thank-you my darling,
I feel so much better.
My troubled heart is now at peace.

Come again, if you would like.
I enjoyed your visit so.
I'll be waiting...

By the swing...
With a rose...
I'll be waiting.

And I'll remember what you said:
Don't forget me.
Don't think without me.
Don't be alone.
Don't be without me.

Don't forget me.

Don't think that I have forgotten you.
Don't think I don't remember.
I do.
I do.
I remember
And
I love you, too.

Don't forget me.

Never, my darling.
I'll see you in my dreams, my love.
I'll see you in my dreams, my friend.
I'll see you in my dreams...
My dreams...
My dreams.

SO I TOLD HER

So I told her once again
For the millionth time
How beautiful she was.

She smiled benignly
With that sad but bemused look in her eye
And said; Thank-you, I know you do.

Which translates to; You're so sweet
And I love you too
But please let's not start lying to one another.

So I told her once again
What talents she possessed.
"You're a true artist," I told her.

And once again she smiled
A simple but bemused denial
... And I sighed.

I told her that she had a lovely voice
And danced like an angel.
She had such natural grace and poise.

It seems that pointing out her grace and poise
Made her self-conscious and
She lost interest in these indulgences.

So I told her that I loved her truly
And that she meant more to me
Than she could ever imagine.

She stared at me rather blankly.
She looked away and then nervously
Looked back towards me once again.

A tear came to her eye.
I'm not entirely sure
But I think she may have believed me.

EYES

I love this poem, not so much for the poem, itself, but for the circumstances that precipitated it.

I was standing in the dollar store, at the Tallahassee Mall. My wife was shopping and I was in my usual daze. I was in one of those pensive, contemplative moods that most would associate with a state of depression. I had withdrawn into myself so deeply my thoughts were echoing inside as if I were in a cavern. My eyes had pulled back so far into my head that I felt that my vision was being obscured by the bony rims of their sockets. There was nothing and no one in this store or mall but myself and a blur of lines and colors, and a background of discordant noises. I associate this state of mind with an exaggerated state of concentration. This is a serious state of 'gonzo.' It can last for hours, and even days. Edgar Allen Poe discussed a state of mind between the unconsciousness of dreams, and the consciousness of waking moments that he described as a creative state. In any case, I was either daydreaming, being creative, or descending into a state of depression, when I felt this pulling or tugging at my sleeve. When I looked, there was this beautiful pair of concerned, loving eyes - a pair of eyes that I had never seen before in my life. They were smiling and then they spoke. "Are you all right?" they questioned. And suddenly I felt warm and alive once again. Were these simply the eyes of beauty, of a transient human being? Or were they the eyes of a transcendent thought, the eyes of the soul of the universe, the eyes of God, possibly? Who did they belong to? Where had they come from? Why did they care about me? For days, and then weeks afterwards, I saw those eyes and the lovely, smiling, concerned face that surrounded them.

She was nothing more than a nice woman, in a department store - her face a bright flower, in a world of blur and haze. She was startling. Since that time I find myself looking into a good many more eyes and more intently. There is something there – even in cats, and dogs, and birds. It's something magical. And oh, how I love the ones that laugh and that aren't afraid. They're a needless, want-less phenomena, that sing with a spirit so beautiful it's blinding. A spirit that can make one wonder if this entire world isn't in fact a delusion designed solely for our personal intrigue and entertainment.

And so I wrote this poem about some of them.

EYES

Eyes!

Excuse me, please? ...
And a hesitant smile,
With a pair of eyes like that of a child.
Thousands and thousands, all cloudy and dark,
Mysterious and frightening.

> a pair in the park
> a life in the dark
> a dollar a pair, for
> a cold blank stare
> a sheet of glass
> a child's 'whoo-ray!'
> a sexy stare
> a menacing glare

a molten hate
swooning, on a swinging gate
a dripping tear
a wanton fear
a pair to love
and another to hug
a pussy cat
a vicious rat
a disappearing cold
with a pair to hold

Eyes!

She is nothing more than a pair of eyes,
Cuddly and warm, powerful and strong,
Wonderfully bright ... heartbreakingly wrong.
The power of poetry, and the wonder of song,
And when they don't see you...

Life is ohh ... so long.

BOYS AND GIRLS

It all begins with little girls who giggle and chide,
And little boys who twiddle and hide.

Then pink bows give way to rosy breasts,
And baseball gloves to hairy chests.

And then it's ... Would you like to dance?
And breathless moments we call romance,

Filled with starry nights and tear filled eyes,
And tender touches with loving sighs.

It's Christmas and candy, and everyone's dream.
It's lipstick and kisses,
It's roses ... it's strawberries and cream;

Followed by golden slippers, and silken veils,
A blushing bride and tuxedo tails.

It's two by two and all that's due,
To a boy and girl in love their whole life through.

Then with hardly a notice,
It's bubbly eyes and goo-goo cries,
It's Mommy ... Daddy, runny noses and teary eyes.

Before you know it,
It's swimming meets, P.T.A., and cookie jars,

Payment books, baiting hooks, and secondhand cars.

Then what do you know, were closing the show,
And all our thoughts are back
To rosy breasts with little pink bows,

And memories of sweet little girls who giggle and chide,
And bashful boys who twiddle and hide.

So squeeze your tickets and hold on tight
To the fleeting moments,
The hugs and kisses,
And those sweet smelling seconds of romantic flight
Through the smiles and tears of life's pale moon light.

JESUS AND THE STARS

No Honey, I don't write poems about Jesus and the stars.
I write more about concrete curbing and secondhand cars.
No Hun, I don't write poems about Jesus and the stars.

I sing my songs about taverns and dimly lit bars.
I wonder about the planets, Sirius and Mars,
But I do my singing about people, railroad tracks and iron
      bars.

No Hun, I no longer write about Jesus and the stars.
Though I often whisper my secrets to empty planets,
Rainbows and distant stars,
I write more about home cooking, pony tails, pretty girls and
      mason jars.

But, no Hon, I no longer write my poems about Jesus and the
      stars.
Though we used to speak and
I've often gone to sleep hugging Venus, Jupiter and Mars;
No Hun, today I don't write poems about Jesus and the stars.

No, I don't write poems about Jesus and the stars.
I write about love and kindness,
But more often, about things the way they are.
No, sweetheart, I no longer write poems about Jesus and the
      stars.

Though for me, it's now a mist of cosmic dust and Milky Way,
I know for you, if you try really, really hard, one day,
You'll be writing beautiful things about Jesus and the Stars
And Heaven, and the Angels, and Jesus and the Stars.
I know you can, and I'll bet you will, one day,
Be writing about the Lord up above,
And all the meanings of love.

I know you can, and I'll bet you will, one day,
Be writing songs about Jesus and the stars,
About moonbeams and Heaven's golden bars,
About love,
And Jesus,
All about Jesus and the stars.

Yes, you'll be singing about Jesus and the Stars,
About Jupiter and Mars,
About the Angels and Heaven,
And Jesus and the Stars.

THE GYPSY

Roaming, roving, singing, sowing, does a gypsy have a soul?
Laughing, crying, stealing, lying, does a Gypsy have a goal?

Lost on the beaches, stuck in the sand,
Telling their fortunes by reading their hand.

He's roamed the world over, a highway his bed,
His family, long lost, they think that he's dead.
He's seen all the sorrow, and roves with a dread.
To the trees and the seas, the Gypsy is wed.

I think I've been born a Gypsy, though my father never knew,
His north, south, east, or west, or whether it was the wind that
    blew.

I think that I'm a Gypsy, because I love to sway
In the steaming perfection of a summer day.
I live to travel, and float with the clouds,
To see the sunsets, and their radiant shrouds.
I dream like a Gypsy, I steal the sky.
I walk over mountains and people ask ... why?

Roaming, roving, singing, sowing, the Gypsies have my soul.
Laughing, crying, stealing, lying, dreaming is my only goal.

They say 'cause I'm a Gypsy I wander without a home.
But, like all the other Gypsies, my home is where I roam.

To breathe the smell of country, to taste the earthy songs,
I sing to the world, "I'm a Gypsy!" and do a tap in my leather
thongs.

Someday you may meet a Gypsy, you will know from the gleam
in his eye ,
That he's tramped the whole world over and exhales with a
Lover's sigh;

"I am a simple Gypsy, but lonely I will not die,
Not as long as there is a sunset to see,
Or a star to rise in the sky."

THOSE SPECIAL MOMENTS

Pay attention!
Pay attention to all those special moments.
Pay attention to the look in his eye.
Pay attention to the feel of her lips.
Pay attention NOW!
Because this 'now' is the stuff of tomorrow's dreams.

Pay Attention now!
Don't miss it! Record it to your memory:
      every touch,
      every embrace,
      ever kind, tender word,
      every uncontrolled laugh,
      every giggle.
Make a mental note.
Paint a mental picture.
Grasp it tight, and hold it ... now!
Because one day it will be all you have.
Pay attention!
      to the smell of her hair.
      the scratch of his beard.
      the feel of her cheek.
      the love in both your eyes.

PAY ATTENTION! ... Don't miss it!
Pay attention to the tickle.
Don't miss the hide and seek.
Pay attention to their shinny eyes

the puckers,
and pouts,
and crocodile tears.
Pay attention to your heart.
Be caring and gentle in deed and thought.
Pay attention...
and be kind to one another.
Pay attention to the most important part.
Pay attention to the tears.
Pay attention to the laughs.
Pay attention to the touching.
Pay attention to the love.

And it will all be easy...
If you pay attention to your heart...
and live it right...
today!

MAKING LOVE

Let's go for a ride on top of the tide.
The darkness is daring and sweet to the touch.
Her fingers ... his stare,
Let's make love ... if we dare.

Let's lay on our backs, naked as the stars up above.
Let's fill this night with the romance of our need for love.
With the help from the smell of the salt from the sea,
We'll make love to an ocean's rolling rhapsody.

A moment like this may never exist.
So grab on, let's reminisce
On the lips of this kiss.

We'll keep ourselves warm
With the breath from our storm.
We'll hold on tight,
Until the world's out of our sight.

Let's make our love
On the crest of an in-coming wave,
Then splash in the sparks
Our fingertips made.

We'll ride this tide with our eyes open wide,
No need to dream or make it seem.
First up with a groan, then down with a moan,
We'll ride this wave's crest, then roll in its foam.

You'll look in his eyes,
Feel the caress of her thighs,
Then swoon in a moon of yearning.

You'll love him again,
And her 'till the end,
In a moment of love ever burning.

You'll touch with your toes;
He'll kiss the red rose,
Of passion's torchless turning.

And she will wreathe with a sigh,
And heave her breasts high,
Then roll in the dream of love's tender churning.

To remember the meaning of a carnal pleading,
To know an evening of lust,
To touch that passion, forever in fashion,
To reel, to feel, to be human,
                    ... Or bust.

TENDERNESS AND TEARS

EDITH

I guess, I thought it would always be,
My life, my health ... my longevity.
I'd never need ... not me ... not I!
I was the kind that would survive.
I'd always be, like I used to be.
Filled with the spirit ... filled with me.

But now, despite myself, it's all gone.
I exist like a rock.
The thought of a stone.
Sleeping ... unknown.

I thought when I reached a point such as this,
I'd tip my hat, and with a shrug and a sigh,
I'd wave to the crowd ... blow a kiss,
And tell the world ... good-bye.

But here I sit as helpless as a child,
Crying all night, and praying for a smile.
I hate to say it ... it makes my ego blush,
But I don't wish for death,
Be it from a bang, or a purr felt hush.

God forgive me, but I'm in no rush.
As bad as it may be
And in this sad state as you can see,
As helpless and dependent, as I may be,
I still long to look out my window and see:

a cat with a string,

a boy with a rope,

a bird with a worm,

a pear with a frost,

a tree with a leaf

a day with a sun,

Or the raindrops, as down my window, they run.

I'm old and as useless as I can be
But I pray ... I honestly pray ...
Please God, can't there just be, a tiny, tiny bit more...
... for me?

WHERE'S OLIVER?

"Where's Oliver?
Have you seen Oliver?
Where's Oliver?"

"She can't find Oliver."

"I know.
It's sad, isn't it?
It seems like she and Oliver were married forever."

"Where's Oliver?
Has anyone seen Oliver?
Where's Oliver?"

"Somebody ought to tell her.
Not to be mean...
Just in a way that she will understand."

"Where's Oliver?
Where is that man?
Where's Oliver?"

"Honey? Come over here and sit down.
Yes, right here at this picnic table.

Oliver died sweetheart.
You know that don't you?

You remember? We had that big funeral?"

"Oliver died?"
"That's right sweetie. You remember now, don't you?"

"Oliver died?"

"Yes! ... Over a year ago.
You remember? ... Remember we had that big funeral?"

The old woman paused, thoughtfully.
She stared off vacantly into the cherry orchard.

She turned and looked into her questioner's eyes.
Her eyes were momentarily thoughtful,
Then slightly tearful.
Then suddenly wide and frightened.

"Wh ... whe ... Where's Oliver?" She asked.

"I don't know sweetie.
Maybe you had best look for him."

The old woman smiled.
"You know, I can never find that man when I want him.
I think I'll keep looking."

"Yes, maybe you'd better."

She rose from the table, then slowly shuffled her bedroom
        slippers
Over the lawn towards their old farm house.

"Where's Oliver?" she cried out, warmly.

"Where's Oliver?

Has anyone seen my Oliver?

Ohhh ... Where's Oliver?"

HAVE YOU COME TO TAKE ME HOME

"Have you come to take me home?" she said.
And the old man began to cry.

"Have you come to take me home?" she said.
And inside he thought he'd die.

"Have you come to take me home?" she said.
She was sick, alone, and misty-eyed.

"Have you come to take me home?" she said.
"Not today, my love, but tomorrow, maybe."

And so he lied.

"Have you come to take me home?" she said.
And then she fell apart.

"Have you come to take me home?" she said.
"My love, my soul, my heart,

The nights here are so long,
And the people cry in their sleep.
I can't eat this food; it's not like home,
And day by day I feel so weak.

Have you come to take me home, my love?
Have you come to take me home?

Have you come to take me home, my love?
                    Or must I die alone?

We've lived this life, just you and I
And now you've put me here to die.
Have you come to take me home, my dear?
Have you come to take me home?

Move closer, closer. Won't you come near, my dear?
I need your hand my love, to chase away this fear.
Help me ... Help me ... You are my only hope."

"I can't bring you home, my dear."
Beside her bed so near, he reached down and took her hand.

"I can't bring you home, my love, though it would be so grand.
If only I could..."
And he caressed and squeezed her hand.

"Have you come to take me home?" she said.
And the old man began to cry.

"Have you come to take me home?" she said.
And inside he thought he'd die.

"Then you're not going to take me home," she spoke.
"Then you're not going to take me home.
You're going to leave me here all by myself;
You're going to leave me here to die alone."

And as she cried, he thought he died

And she pulled her hand from his.
But he pulled it back and put on it a kiss.

She struggled and struggled as a weak one might,
But she was old, sick, and weary from fright.
He struggled with her, there, all night,
To keep her hand with his,
And stood beside her bed and cried,
Until, at last, she finally died.

"Have you come to take me home, my love?
 Have you come to take me home?"

"No, my dear, but I'll be near
You'll never be alone.

You'll never be alone, my love,
You'll never be alone."

JACK SPRAT

I knew Jack for a number of years. I always felt that Jack could have been the inspiration for the original Sad Sack cartoon strip. He was a "sorry" type fellow. He seemed to have just enough ambition to keep breathing. That's providing there was no serious obstruction to that circumstance. He was kind of like Forest Gump, but without the good fortune. He did some commercial shrimping and some oystering. He liked to fish with nets, poles or whatever. He fished the gulf, the bay, the rivers, the creeks, and the ditches. He enjoyed fishing with a cane pole, and had a passion for Bream.

I lived next to him at this campground. He rented an old camper - the kind that slid onto the bed of a pickup truck. This one didn't have a pickup truck; it just sat on an array of concrete blocks.

This poem began at the Eastpoint, post office. He was picking up his mail ... general delivery. He couldn't afford a box. He told me that he wasn't feeling well. He had been to the V. A. hospital. He couldn't go there often because it was too far away. Jack was a veteran of the Vietnam War. From then on I saw him here and there fishing, but each time I saw him he got thinner, and he looked worse and worse. He was like a stray cat with a deathly virus - everybody looked at him, but nobody ever stopped to pet him.

Jack, I always felt, was the kind of guy who didn't really deserve to die. I mean, for some people, death is a conclusion. As they say today, their death was a sort of justification, a closure. For some their death seems to serve as some sort of example, or moral lesson. For others death seems to be just what they have been looking for. Then there are those of whom we say there was no person that we ever met who was more deserving. But Jack didn't deserve to die one way or another. He was just here. He wasn't in anybody's way, and if he was, I am sure that he would have moved. He didn't bother anybody. He drank a little and fished a lot. He had no real opinions on anything, and always seemed to have a reasonable amount of compassion for anybody and anything. His dying served no real purpose, but I suppose, some would say, neither did his living. In this respect, I guess, he was pretty much like the most of us.

JACK SPRAT

Jack Sprat could eat no lean.
He didn't have money for a packet of beans.
He worked enough to live in a truck,
And he drank a bit when he was down on his luck.

He was up or down, and roved about town.
He wore old clothes, but never a frown.
Jack Sprat, he ate no fat,
And his mother doesn't know or care where he's at.

Jack had no use for fancy things,
Diamonds, or jewels, or sapphire rings.
He sat on the bank and fished for Bream,
And the cancer made him slim and trim.

And when he died, no one cried.
Some shook their heads, and a few of them lied.

"He was a hell of a man, a really brave fellow."
But the truth was
He was kind of 'wussy' and rather mellow.

Jack rarely sat in a pew with a hymn.
He just sat on the bank and tried to catch Bream.
He never owned, himself, a good pair of shoes,
And he never got done payin' his dues.

He was always going to get him a car,
But, really, he had no need to travel that far.
He mostly stayed on the unpaved street,
With sand in his toes and dirt on his feet.

He never went out to try to win.
He mostly sat on the bank and tried to catch Bream.
And when the cancer caught him and made him so thin,
He just sat on the bank and caught some Bream.

And when he died ... no one cried.
Oh his mother frowned, and his father sighed.
But I swear, when I saw him in his box,
He had a little grin, and, I know darn straight,
He was sitting on some bank,
Trying to catch him some Bream.

RAY

It's 2:30 in the morning and I can't sleep.
I'm staring at the darkness
And listening to the echoing hospital sounds.

I hear people groaning,
And some whimpering in their sleep.
I want to jump up and get out of here.

I want to pull all these tubes and plugs.
I want to go for a walk down Broadway.
I can't stop thinking about the wife, my kids,
And all my old pals.

Everybody has dropped by.
They all have that look in their eye.
Memories ... a million memories.

One minute I'm a kid again
Hangin' out on the corner,
And the next, I'm "Mister Dolan,"
The old buck at third base
On the kids little league field.

I think of all the laughs...
All the good times,
And instead of laughing,
Tears fill my eyes
And I get a lump in my throat.

I don't know what the heck I'm crying about.
I guess that it is because I know that I'm dying,
But I just don't know how...

I just don't know how to do it.

GOOD-BYE MAMA

She was so beautiful.
I loved her so.
She was so shy.
Almost anything could make her cry.
She was so shy.
Too shy, I guess, to be alive.

She read to me from stories old,
From ancient days, about tombs of gold.
Oh god ... I loved her so.

She loved me.
She told me many times.
She told me, and she showed me.
She was so dear ... I loved her so.

She cried at the movies.
She cried reading poems.
I cried when she died.
And oh ... how I miss her so.

The wheel fell off the grocery cart.
If only she could disappear.
I was only playing.
She was so embarrassed.
If only she could disappear.
And so she has...
$\qquad$ forever.

I loved her so.
Her eyes so sweet and caring.
Her touch so soft and kind.
She was so sweet ... I loved her so.
I thought that I could never let her go.

I hugged her there.
I hug her now.
How strange, how ugly, how cold,
Never again would I be so old.
I breathed air that was meant for her,
And cried mother ... mother ... mother.

Good-bye my love.
Good-bye to all our schemes and plans.
Good-bye to tender, lifeless hands.
Good-bye to all the dreams untold.
Good-bye Mama, you'll never grow old,
And I will always love you so.

ALL GOD'S CHILDREN

A young man came into my place of business. It was obvious that he had one of those diseases with the long names and weird symptoms. Just standing still his body jerked, his eyes blinked, his head snapped from one side to another. When he sat down, a leg would occasionally jerk out into the air or an arm would shoot off in any direction.

He was a friendly young fellow and he wanted to talk. The room was filled with costumers who were eating their lunch or having dessert. When this young boy began talking, everyone else stopped. For whatever reasons they all wanted to listen to what the poor fellow had to say. They would glance up over a spoon full of ice cream or peek from out the corner of their eye.

All through this conversation I kept trying to think positive thoughts. I mean God has a reason for everything, right? This boy and this disease have a positive function, of course. I mean God doesn't play dice with his poor creatures, does he? But the more I talked and observed this man, the more agnostic I became. I could find no acceptable rationalization for this young man's problem. If this was one of God's little jokes, it wasn't very funny. If God is trying to tell me something, he could have chosen a kinder way. But then of course, how many are there out there who would feel very, very lucky to be blessed with this poor boy's simple affliction. And then, of course it goes without saying, that there for the grace of God go I. My conclusion was that this young man was simply another one of God's creatures, and the rightness or wrongness of it all will have to left to His conscience.

ALL GOD'S CHILDREN

"I I I I'm on the fah fah fah fire department,"
He said with a shocking twitch and grimace.
"See my ba ba badge?"
He pointed to a shiny, silver-red badge pinned to his T-shirt.
"I'm a va va volunteer on the fire department.
I think that I am going to go to ca ca college."
He twitched. His whole body then jerked, as if shot electrically.
"I don't know why a person couldn't go tah tah college
If he has already graduated from
Hah hah high school. Do you?"

"I don't see why not."

"I think that I I I am goin' to go to fah fah Fire Fighter College.
I wah wash dishes at the restaurant.
My fah fah friend at the fah fah fah fire department says
That he would never wah wah wash dishes.
But I don't care what he says
Because it's a job, and hah hah having a job
Is better than not hah hah having a job."

"That's right. You are a pretty smart fellow."

"I got an alligator in the pond in front of my house.
I called the Conservation.
They said that the alligator wasn't bah bah bothering nobody,
So I should leave it alone.
But I told them ... what about all the lah lah little kids

116

That go there fah fah fishin'?
And what about their little pa pa pets?"

"And what did they say to that?"
His body jerked again, electrically,
And one arm shot up over his head.

"Nuh nuh nothin' … but I'll tell you wah wah what…
I'm gonna get my Four-ten, and when that alligator
Pops up its head…
I'm gah gah gonna let it have it … both barrels!"

"You're gonna kill it?"

"Well, I don't like tah tah do that…
Bah bah but…"

"Maybe, you shouldn't do that."

"Maybe I wah wah won't, but I'll tell you wah what …
If I go out fishin' and I catch one of them thirty-six
Inch red fish … you can bet
I ain't gonna throw him back.
I don't care wah wah what the Conservation says.
I'm carryin' him up tah tah the house."
Both his arms jerked spastically,
And then one leg shot out straight.

"You gonna kill it?"

"Wah wah well, I don't like to kill it…
I don't like to kill nothin'…

Bah bah but I have to kill it if I want to eat it?"

"Yes you do."

"Yes I do ... I hah hah have to do it.
Sometimes you hah hah have to do things
That you don't like to do.
But you hah hah have to?"

"I know."

AFTER WE'VE GONE OUR SEPARATE WAYS

I'm very sure about falling in love, and the universal nature of the event, but I'm not so sure about falling out of love.

I've heard people say that eventually they just fell out of love. I wonder?

I don't think that I have ever lost love. Any love that has ever been given to me, graciously, seems to be forever there within me, and I can call the moments of it up to recollection at will.

I can remember today the loving laugh and joyous sparkle from the longest, most distant moments of my life. I can feel yet, on my cheek, the moistness of lips that are at this moment, at best, flecks of dust in a fleshless grave. I can still feel about me the warmth of embraces that were only intended in the thoughts and eyes of those who have once loved me. If you have ever, even mistakenly, loved someone for even a fraction of a second, I think that they, and you, will - as long as you both are - posses the warmth and beauty of that feeling within yourselves.

It hurts to lose something, or someone that you have loved, but I know that as long as I am, they are; and that tenderness once given will always be a precious part of oneself, and for those to whom you have given love it will be with them for as long as they remain in existence. So I am not afraid to be loved or to give love because I have learned that a little love can last, at minimum, one lifetime, and at best, for as long as creatures, possessive of the spirit, continue to share in the wonder of the exchange.

AFTER WE'VE GONE OUR SEPARATE WAYS

When we've gone our separate ways,
And the years are all yesterdays,
Will you see a pair of loving eyes,
And then remember mine?
When we've gone our separate ways,
And the tomorrows that were once ours
Are all just lost todays,
Will you awake from a warm dream of love,
Then sit alone in the darkness and remember me in your arms?

When we've gone our separate ways,
And the years are all yesterdays
And the tomorrows that once were ours
Are all just lost todays,
Will you remember that I really did love you?
That you were all my dreams come true?
Will you think kind thoughts
And spare me a smile or two?
Will you love me for just a second,
Because I will always be in love with you...
Even after we've gone our separate ways.

I'll remember the feel of your lips,
And the smell of your hair.
I'll remember the tone of your voice
When you still loved me and you still cared.

But for now I want us to go our separate ways
Before the coolness in your eyes kills me,
And turns all my loving sighs into wishful good-byes.

But when we've gone our separate ways
If you see me walking,
Don't cross the street or drop your hat over your eyes
And pretend that we never met.
Let's be nice, and remember that a million years ago
We looked into each others eyes
And breathed each other's sighs.

So when we've gone our separate ways
And all our memories are yesterdays,
Let's remember the plans that we once made.
Let's remember the loving moments
In the cool green shade.

When we've gone our separate ways
And all our years are yesterdays,
And the tomorrows that once were ours
Are all just lost todays,
Remember that I really did love you.
You were all my dreams come true.
Think kind thoughts...
Spare me a smile or two ...
Love me for just a second ...
Because I will always be in love with you,
Even after we've gone our separate ways.

ISN'T THERE ALWAYS ANOTHER DREAM

But isn't there always another dream?
No matter how twisted and distorted everything may seem
Isn't there always another dream?

When all that ever was, or mattered ... isn't.

When everyone who ever cared ... doesn't.

When all you thought there ever was ... really wasn't.

Isn't there always another dream?

Isn't there always that faint, faint gleam
That tells you, somehow, that you have to dream?

And don't you really want to live?
Even though you know that you have nothing left to give.
Don't you really want to live?

When you could just crawl up into a corner and cry.

When you even hope and pray to die.

Don't you know inside...it's a lie?
And don't you really want to live?

When all that ever was, or mattered ... isn't.

When everyone who ever cared ... doesn't.

When all you thought that there ever was ... really wasn't.

Isn't there always another dream?

Isn't there always that faint, faint gleam

That tells you somehow...

That you have to dream?

BUT, DO YOU LOVE ME

But, do you love me?
And how would I know?
I look into your eyes, but the love doesn't show.
So how ... how would I know?
Days and nights, weeks and years,
Moments of laughter, and a lifetime of tears.

But, do you love me?
And how would I know?
Nothing I see would tell me it's so.
We touch, we love, we laugh, we smile.
We cherish the memories, mile after mile.

But, do you love me?
And how would I know?
Unless once in a while...
You'd tell me so.

ON THE

SERIOUS

SIDE

BOMBS ARE DROPPING

Bombs are dropping, but I can't hear a thing.
Bombs are dropping, I can feel them ring.
BOOM! ... BOOM! ... BOOM! ...
See everything crumble.
Buildings tumble, the ground's a rumble.

Bombs are dropping, but I can't hear a thing.
BOOM! ... BOOM! ... BOOM!
Bombs are dropping, I can feel them ring.
I can hear them whistle. I can hear them sing.
But yet, but yet ... I can't hear a thing.

Buildings are falling and crashing to the ground.
Children are screaming and running around.
But I'm all right in my suit and tie.
I've got my briefcase, and can't seem to cry.

Bombs are dropping...
BOOM! ... BOOM! ... BOOM!
I'm cleaning up destruction with my little whisk-broom.
Hear them whistle ... hear them sing.
Bombs are dropping, but I can't hear a thing.

BOMBS ARE DROPPING!
BOMBS ARE DROPPING!
BOOM! ... BOOM! ... BOOM!
But I can't hear a thing.

HERE I AM ALIVE

It's funny.

Here I am alive,
And tomorrow I'm going to die,
And nobody knows
That I have ever actually been here.
Nobody knows me.

It is like I sneaked in over the fence
When the world was closed.
I stood on the field.
I held the ball.
I played the game.
But the roaring crowd never was,
And no one saw me.

I've been here ... and there,
And nobody has seen me come or go.
And when I die,
Nobody will care, or ask God why.

I've worked like a fool,
And I haven't accomplished a darn thing.
I haven't been here.

I've hidden myself away, inside.

And here I am alive

And tomorrow I'm going to die,

And nobody will know

That I've ever actually been here.

And sometimes, I wonder.

Is there anyone who will really care?

IT IS NOT FAIR

It is not fair,
And you know it as well as I do.
Yet here we sit,
As if our hands were tied behind our backs.

It's not fair,
And you know it as well as I.
So why do we try to justify it all?
It is not fair today;
It wasn't fair yesterday;
And it won't be fair tomorrow.

So what is the argument?
Unfair should remain unfair?
Right and wrong are inconsequential?
It is not anyone's fault?
It is beyond rectification?
Justice should not be our standard;
Order - would be more appropriate?
It is just the way things are?

Don't ask me,
Bring your complaints to the Responsible Party.
If we all do what we must do,
Then who is left to do what should be done?
I don't have the time;
You don't have the inclination;
Together we don't have the money

Or the means?

So?

It doesn't get solved.

It is never rectified.

It all continues as it always has.

It is the dust beneath our beds.

Are there any debts to be paid for this indifference?

Who is there righteous enough to demand payment?

No one knocks on my door.

Sad faces stare wide-eyed and bewildered.

Their tears say;

It is not fair.

IT IS SO REGRETTABLE

It is so regrettable.
I feel so very, very sad.
It's so very, very regrettable.
I know that you do not understand my feeling
In this regard,
But it is so regrettable,
So very, very regrettable.
I have thought about it so many, many times.
But it never seems to get any better.
It's regrettable.

I try, sometimes, not to think about it.
I try to laugh and be happy.
But then there it is
Buried deep in the back of my mind.
Deep.
It is very deep.
And the only thing that I can say is:

It is so regrettable.
It is so very, very regrettable.
I really don't know why it must be this way.
It is not necessary,
But yet,

It is so regrettable.
It never seems to end.
It will not go away.

It goes on, and on, and on, and on.

If I could make it stop, you know that I would,
But ... but, it is beyond me.
It leaves me speechless,
And all that I can think is:

Why is it all so regrettable?
Why must it all be so regrettable?
In any case,
I suppose that I will say good-bye now.
What else can I do?

I don't make the decisions.
I'm simply here.
And I will be very honest with you, I find it all

So very, very regrettable.
I hope that you can forgive me.
I wish that I had a better way with words.
But, all I can think to say is:

I find it all so regrettable,
So very, very regrettable.
I wish you all well
Wherever you go.

But while you are all here, let me tell you, sincerely,
I wish you the best,
And I do find it all very regrettable.
Thank - you.

IT'S TOO HARD

It is so hard.
It is oh so terribly hard.
It's too hard.

I've tried.
I've tried so hard.
But it's too hard.
It's too, too hard.

I've worked so hard.
But it is too hard.
It is too, too hard.

It mattered once.
It mattered too much.
It mattered too, too much.

Oh how it mattered.
It was life or death.
It mattered to me.
It really, really mattered.

But, no more, for
It is too hard.
It was too, too hard.
It was too hard for me.

You were too hard.

You were too, too hard.
You were too hard for me.

And now it doesn't matter.
Once it mattered.
But, it matters no more.
Because it was too hard.

It was too, too hard.

Now I'm too old.
And it doesn't matter
Maybe it never mattered.

I did want it so.
I wanted it so badly.
I wanted it oh so badly.

But it was too hard.
It was too, too hard.
It was oh so very hard

You made it too hard.
You made it too, too hard.
You made it too hard for me

Too ... too ... hard.

MR. NOBLE REGRETS

It was the most unrewarding, unfulfilling
Thing that I have ever done.

Why I devoted so much of my life to it
I will never understand:

For the most part
It only made me miserable.

It didn't do much
For anyone else either.

I should have just ignored the whole thing
And let it die.

Who would believe all the time
And all the hours?

For a time
It was my whole life.

Every waking moment
Was spent thinking, preparing, anticipating.

I thought it to be the most important
Thing in all of life.

If I had never given it one second
My life would have been more rewarding.

But for that time it became more important to me
Than life itself.

I wouldn't be able to live without it,
I thought.

But live I did;
And life was better.

It was easier to handle, more sensible,
More focused and more realistic.

Not being able to let it go, I think,
Made me into a creature other than myself at times.

When I reflect upon it now
I can't imagine what I was thinking.

I made myself miserable
And for no reason whatsoever.

I say that I won't ever let it happen again
But, you know, I think it is happening again

Right now.

SPONTANEOUS NOTHING

I'm trying to write a poem without thought;
Spontaneous nothing.
Because even thinking becomes a bore.
Thinking is so ... thought-like.
Thinking is so rational, so sensible.
People tire of correct thinking.
They want to escape to witches
     and flying brooms
     and rooms the color of the wind
     bugs that dance
     and animals that talk.

Sensible thought is so ordinary,
So matter of fact.
It leaves no room for creative mis-being,
In-cognitive wonder and impossible what-ifs.
We have the un-real, the un-born, and the unfathomable.
We have anti-gravity, and anti-matter.
In the world of the un-thought
Anything can be taught.
Nothing is not impossible.
Nothing is, in fact, fact.
All is not all.
Empty can be full.
A top can have no bottom.
We can have two everythings;
And they can be beside one another ... and different.
We can have opposing similarities,

Negative positives and passive aggressives.
Apples can be compared with oranges.
The sick can be the healthy;
And the wealthy can be the poor.

It is like listening to Jazz and the discordant note.
The note that binds is the note that doesn't fit.
What doesn't follow is what should be next.
So let's not think and let us see what happens.

Or ... is that the way it has always been.

THE FACE AT THE WINDOW

She saw in his eyes all of her dreams.
She was sweet and kind and bursting at the seams.
She was as pretty as can be, with those eyes of brown,
As she danced and sparkled on her night on the town.

It pains like a dagger ... twisting ... twisting...
And waits like a child lost in the night.
She peeks from the window, with tears of fright,
And she cries and cries, until he's left her sight.

And her Hell sits comfortably blazing in the lap of the sun,
While heaven drifts, aimlessly, among the stars,
And the dream smothers the real,
And the truth is lost, somewhere, out in the sky.
And there is no answer to her questions...

... Just her sigh.

WHO AM I?

"What are you?" they ask.

I'm an open wound, I tell them.
I'm a pain that will never subside.
I'm the pity filled tear
In the corner of your eye.
I'm the sorrow and the sadness.
I'm the horror and the shame.
I'm the child that never grew up.
I'm freedom in your cage.

"What are you?" they ask.

I'm the weed in your garden.
I'm the flower growing in the rock.
I'm the truth that you are unwilling to face.
I'm reality in your face.

"Who are you?" they ask.

I'm the beaten and the abused.
I'm the worthless and the used.
I'm what you were...
Before you became what you are.

"But, what are you?" they ask.

I'm death and dying.

I'm old and weary.
I'm all the things
That you would like to hide or forget.

But yet...
I'm all that makes existence worthwhile.
Without me,
Even you could never be.

SCARLET LETTER

I wear the Scarlet Letter,
But it's sown into my heart.
None of you can see it,
But it keeps us far apart.

I try to hide, or look the part,
But I often fear you see it.
Then my face turns red,
And I hide my head.
Oh my lord, how I wish to be dead.

I wear a Scarlet Letter,
And it is sown into my heart.
The stitches, they are bleeding;
Of sweet tenderness, I'm needing.

I wear a Scarlet Letter,
And it's sown into my heart.
My eyes bear the burden;
My soul gives it start.

I wear a Scarlet Letter,
And it is sown into my heart.
It's my secret, never ending,
And it keeps us far apart.

Oh God I curse this letter,
That I've sown into my heart.

But God, He can't release me.
His love seems to decrease me.
I must myself police me;
For I have sown this letter,
With rawhide stitches better;
Yes, I have sown this letter;
This horrid Scarlet Letter;
This painful pure blood letter;
Yes, I have performed this treason;
I am the truth and reason;

I'm the horrid tailor;
I'm the toughened sailor,
Who has patched this sordid letter;
There is no treason better;
I have sown this Scarlet Letter to my heart.

MOTHERS AND SONS

Scowling faces with gaping jaws.
Those sunken eyes, with that look ... lost and far,
The back of a hand and a shrieking scream,
The hate! The power!

An ugly love for an ugly child...
An ugly love and a child gone wild.

The unkempt hair and the twisting nervous fingers,
The jitters ... she's got the jitters.
She's up, she's down...
She's around and around.

She's a mother ... the Mother of hate.
She's a mother ... the Mother of disgust.
She's a mother ... "The" Mother!
But her child's a bust.

She's a mother ... a mother of anger ... a mother of lust.
She lusts! She lusts!
She reeks with self pity...
Self pity and disgust!

She talks and she cries,
She lives and she hides.

She's vicious!

And late in the night,
In the quiet and the dark,
She sits on my bed.

Her smile's a leer...
And her teeth are fangs.
She wants to bite me.
She wants to bite me...
And she says that it's love.
And when she chokes me...
She says it's a hug.

She tears at my flesh, then devours my heart.
She's a wild animal, a pack of beasts!
My blood drips from her fangs.
She has the meat of my heart between her teeth.
But she's a mother ... a Mother...

And I'm her son.

I'M A STUBBORN OLD MULE

I'm a stubborn old mule,
As stubborn as they come.
A rail between the eyes is the only thing
That'll make me run.

He doesn't pat me gently on the brow,
Or say, "Come now friend, a little further now."
No, No! It's a beam between the eyes,
And a roaring scream and cry,
As he pushes and shoves with venom for an eye,
And brutality frothing in his unpatient sigh.

He has no memory of the burden I bore,
When I carried him, his gold, and a mountain of store.

He forgets how on the side of cliffs I trod,
As he cowered and crazed and cursed his God.

He has no memory of the thirst I craved,
Carrying his drink to an early grave.
He's a brave man, who went down in books,
A crusty determined miner.
And I, who braved his dirty looks,
Hefted the load of gold for my forty-niner.

Ah yes, a brave man was he,
But he wouldn't have a nickel if it weren't for me.

But I'm a stubborn old mule,
And as dumb as can be.
But the old bastard wouldn't have a nickel,
If it weren't for the likes of me.

Carried him where his pretty horses wouldn't go,
Through mountains, and deserts, and fields of snow.
But, in his fancies, he dreams of a saddle
And a golden mane,
His pretty little horses,
Dining on sacks of expensive grain.

But for his trusty, dusty steed, forever at his side,
It's a drunken mumble, and tempered lash,
And another scar in my hide.

Many a day, when I'd had enough,
I sat in the middle of the road,
And laughed as he stammered and huffed and puffed.
Oh, how he wished to shoot me...
But who would carry the load?

Yes, many a time I wouldn't go on.
But does he remember how I danced
On the edge of a cliff,
As he trembled and gasped, and for his life hung on.
A man of might, and right and power and gain,
And as he drunk his whiskey and barked to the stars,
I stood by quietly in the snow and the rain.

I'm as stubborn as a mule,
As stubborn as they come.
A rail between the eyes is the only thing
That'll make me run.

I carry his load, sure footed I go,
But when I've had enough of his rum drenched batter,
I pull up, take a seat, and listen to his chatter.

The other day, in a fit of rage,
He pulled his rifle from my side.
"Move along, you stubborn old bastard,
Or I'll shoot you right here,
And then tan your damn hide."

I yawned, then lifted my head and brayed.
I curled my lips, then bared my broken teeth.
And when he shouldered his gun, I stared into the breech.
I felt the powder as it burnt my eye,
And a dull thud as a jolt from hell pierced my skull,
And I fell there onto my side.

But I'm a stubborn old mule,
As stubborn as they come.
I laid there with his pack and store,
And stared up at his eye.
And I'm proud to say, I hung there waitin' to die,
Long enough to see the dumb bastard
Put down his rifle and cry.

Yes, I'm a stubborn old mule,
As stubborn as they come.
It takes a rail between the eyes
To get me up to run.
But when you have a load too tough to hold,
It's a call for the likes of me.
And I bear it well, sure footed and determined,
Right to the rim of hell.
But what he can't stand,
Is that I'm a bit of a man.
And, as the man, I have my pride,
And how I tried, and tried, and tried.
But, oh how glad I am that when I came to die
I was beast enough to make the bastard cry...
Yes, beast enough...
To make that bastard cry.

CALL OF THE DEAD

As I pulled each foot, pace after pace,
And drudged about the yard,

Hating, despising, but keeping my place,
And finding it increasingly hard.

I pulled my bitterness up from the pace,
And stared at the spacious sky.

The hate siphoned down to the tips of my toes,
And fancies shrouded my head.

Though not in the least did it assuage my woes,
For hatred is never dead.

"Follow the song of the dead," they said.
"Follow the song of the dead.
The dead are the spirits who know, yes know…
The dead are the spirits who know."

I just walked in rank while my spirit sank,
And my head began to bob.

But as the pavement slipped, and the leather gripped,
They were only doing their job.

Their job … it was, to keep us in step…
Step, upon step, upon step.

Step to the pace ... the pace of a race...
They're only doing their job.

I turned from the thought which cruelty wrought
And returned my head to the sky.

But upon this thought, my vision caught
The horror of those who die.

And now entwined with the song of the dead,
An apparition before my eye...

All ragged, worn and weary souls
Were marching across the sky.

"Come join the ranks of the dead," they said.
"Come ... join us rancorous dead."

And on they marched, across the sky,
A line which had no end,
Moaning, and groaning, with ghoulish cry,
The rancorous song of the dead.

"The dead are the spirits who know, yes know...
The dead are the spirits who know."

I closed my eye to the specter nigh,
And frantically shook my head.

But in my ears, yet, the lingering cries,
In the raucous tone of the dead.

"Follow the song of the dead," they said.
"Follow the song of the dead."

With averted eye, I shunned their cry,
As yet they marched over head.

I chained my pace, and firmed my step,
Fearing to loose the beat.

One and two ... one and two...
Conform you feet to the beat.

I walked and walked, it seemed like miles,
Avoiding their deathly smiles.

But then as I looked, aside of my foot,
Another was pacing the same.

With horror, I shook, as his hand he put,
And cooled my sweating palm.

With a frigid flame, he called my name.
He tugged and yanked at my arm.

I confused my step, then shuffled from harm
And joined again with the real.

But with a voice that quelled,
I heard him yell;

"You're just a spoke in a wheel.
You may march away and avoid our song,
But shortly your heart will swell.
Never can you march away from the throng,
And pass by the flames of Hell."

With a demon-faced fear, I remember his sneer,
As he rejoined the ranks of the dead.
He was last in line ... then the skies turned clear,
And my face from white to red.

Well, that was a day I won't forget,
And here I am marching again.

The sky is bright, and my spirits light.
It's the happiest day of the year.

Above my head, there's a cloudy bed,
And everything seems so dear.

A smile on my face, as I skip to the pace,
Mocking that ghoulish sneer.

With fences around, and the treacherous sound,
Flowing beyond the barbed wire,

I laugh at the race, and grin at the face,
As marching we tramp by the mire.

The soggy and snake ridden mire...
That offers no hope or desire.

But as I walk, I hear the clock, cracking away like fire.
But oh, not again! ... It can't be again! ...
And I turned my head to the clouds.
A huge mass of white, towering in height,
Sailing across the sky.
Like a desert of white, on a sea of night,
It brings me a breathless sigh.
It's motion aloft, so flowing and soft,
Beckons me to its choir.
My head, it spins, as my heart it wins,
And I dance to the glorious choir.

But then a dull tick-tock, as I hear the clock,
And my feet head for the mire.
The guard screams ... "Halt! ... It isn't my fault!"
And now I'm before the barbed wire.
The clouds they beam like a cascade of dreams,
As I watch them float up higher.
"HALT OR I'LL SHOOT!"
And the whistles, they toot...
"HALT OR I'LL BE FORCED TO FIRE!"
But my feet had no fault as they mocked the assault,
And climbed the treacherous barbed wire.
"To freedom!" they sing.
"We'll fly you right over the mire."

Well, as the clouds ... they dance,
My feet ... they prance, and the guns begin to fire.
But with a few more steps ... just a few more steps,
I'll be slouching my way through the mire.

Then I heard a ringing, and angels singing.
And as I followed the clouds ahead,
It seems the voice of Destiny's choice,
Chanted to me and said;
"Turn yourself around, and see what you've found."
And there, I saw myself ... dead.
Floating in the mire, my body swept higher,
As they lifted me from my bed.
The sky all red, in torrents it bled,
Like my body afloat on the mire.

Then, back through the gate enclosed by the wire.
Watching my body with dread,
I heard the beat ... the beat ... of the feet ... of the dead...
And that same ghoulish voice ... it said;

"Come follow the song of the dead," he said.
"Come follow the song of the dead.
The dead are the spirits who know, yes know.
The dead are the spirits who know."

"You've joined the ranks of the dead," they all said.
"You've joined the ranks of us ... dead."

FIRST LINE INDEX

www.ingramcontent.com/pod-product-compliance
Lightning Source LLC
Chambersburg PA
CBHW072012040426
42447CB00009B/1592